This collection of poems is dedicated to my family

CONTENTS

1 SPECTRES

Sometimes I remember dead voices
Bodiless but connected
Within a dark warmth, frozen
Most are troubled, some yearn
But I can in a moment
Obliterate them
Turning their sounds into shadows
Bury them in blackness
Forgetful
But nothing lasts
Eventually free
They will be
Once again my ghosts.

2   KEYBOARD ME

Keyboard me
A punch without pain
Stable and static
Error and Delete
Undo, start over
Correct.

3   THE WHISPERING WHISTLER

The Whispering Whistler
Rustles
Remembrances
Reaching
Or
Retching out
Things
I never wanted
And can't hand back.

4 LORELEI

Lorelei, Lorelei
Now only a myth to me

Lorelei, Lorelei
Now I am free

Lorelei, Lorelei
Where is your voice and your siren song?

Lorelei, Lorelei
You are now all but gone

Lorelei, Lorelei
Within the silence that now remains

Lorelei, Lorelei
I no longer feel the sharp pains

Lorelei, Lorelei
A voice in the deep

Lorelei, Lorelei
Sleeping you shall keep.

5   PATTERNS

Patterns
   H
   A
   P
   Everything

Patterns
   H
   O
   U
   L
   Demonstrate

Patterns
   L
   I
   Past

Repeat………………..

6   FORGOTTEN?

He was a martyr
She was moral
They never forgot
He gave it up
She surrendered
They laboured
He was penitent
She was true
They are no more
We forget
He knew

7 BETWEEN NOW AND THEN

Between now and then
LIES
A sharp critical divide

You were better then
You should by now

An ocean connects
Hope's island beacon
Lit and flaming
From
Reality's tattered, battered
Sure

8 AUDIENCE OF ONE

Moments mine
Entwined neatly
Secretly together
Tethered by
My own
Grown
Inner living light.

9 MACHINE

Mechanical man
Made in a mechanical age
A conglomeration of mechanisms
A ticking clock.

I was the machine
Biologically conceived
Built from Historio-political and socio constructs in flux
A psychological amalgam of influences large and small
A human animal

I believed in death
and man
In knowledge and understanding
In the random and explainable.
Positions empirically provided
And dialectically provable.

A machine for thinking
A machine for feeling
A machine.

Then
I surrendered to the mystery
And freedom

10　WHAT REMAINS?

Words are mayflies
Poetry elegant vapours

Actions are monuments
Ozymandias

Listen

11   PERMANENCE TEMPORAL

In our lives
All seems now
All seems today
Yet we flow
Within the future
At the brink
of our past

12   MEMORY

Subliminal shadows
Erupting from
Collected cadences

Sounds collective
Mostly forgotten
But   never lost

Sometimes emergent
From blank forgetfulness
A word, or phrase

Symphonic river
Each note, H20
Each year, a torrent

Surging
Exciting
Urgent

Ssssh
Fading
But not forgotten

Shifting momentary moments
Remembered somehow
Recalled sometimes

Waters salient
with sight and sound
with sensation and soul.

13   DRINKING FROM LETHE'S CUP

Darkly a midnight shines, dazzling with regretted evils
Hidden within the crackles of reminiscence
Harbingers sharply revile, calling and berating

I want to drink forgetful
of my name

The worst of me whatever clings
Like a stink
Sin has been with me so long
That I can never lose it

Patterns now seem beyond correction
Give me a draft of forgotten
To drink deep and cleanse
To start again innocent

But I am man and I will sin again and again and again.
How do I transcend?
Forgive me!?
Yet, I can not myself do so

14   BLACK BLOSSOM

Black Blossom
Teenage spring
Dark Dreams
Am I depraved or deprived?

Black Blossom
Sweet
Black Blossom falling

Black Blossom
Petals a pitch carpet
Growth
Summer forgetfulness

15 QUESTION

Message
Select
Write message

R you u?
Or r u ?

Send.

16   I DREAMT OF LOST SOULS

Last night I dreamt of lost souls
Souls lost to me
Shades that walked in flesh
Only in my dream

They were once.
Now a mirage
A reflection in sub consciousness
Each voice, face, figure
A longing

Can't have them
Sometimes shouldn't

A city
Half remembered
Half imagined

A theatre
A production
Half understood
Joy and grief
Wanting
Where the allusion tantalises

Suppression
The grand illusion for which dreams were born
Resolution
A luxury for the living.

17   VERSION ?

Self image
Vision?
Nightmare ?

Hero
Zero

Saint
Sinner

Man
Sham

All

18 BOY TO MAN

When I was Robin Hood
In a Lincoln Green World
All was Merry Men
Dancing Quarterstaffs
Fizzing Fun
When I was Robin Hood

19   END OF INNOCENCE

I had forgotten the day I started to die
Fear and truth
A tsunami unstoppable filling every space
Drowning innocence

The day I started to die
The day of realisation
A remorseless sensation
A child abandoning immortality
Growing and dying.

Dying so long now that I forgot
The day it started
And the birth of mortality

The first day I prayed.
The first day alone.
The start of the end
of childhood days.

20 DREAMS

Time fills the hunger of aspiration
And I forget the
Boy drenched with notions
Soaked in ideas
Childhood the monsoon of dreams

Though fantasies never fade
Possibilities are lost one by one
Probability curves away

21 NIGHT RAIN AND DRIVING

Multi coloured rain
Dribbling in through memories
Open window
Pushing through streets at night
Dad driving

Born again
I'm child
pungent reminiscence

I should be this
Living dream
Caught in time between lives
Just here and being

22 TRANQUILITY

In my head
The tide laps
Against a
Perfect shore.

I can't
Reach its
Purity

I manage
Only the
Staccato
Stuttering
of my own
imperfect
Attempts to
Wash ashore

A blind mariner.
Childhood anchoring
To a compass point
Alone in darkness;
Illuminated by
Sensations in time.

Where is the island   of tranquillity?
Its peaceful landscape verdant
With my own essential being
That time's tempest robbed.

23 WAR

Did you forget?
Your severed hand
Your slashed face
Your burnt stump
Your orphaned child
Your raped wife
Your abandoned soul
Again.

24 I BELIEVE

I believe
Is that whimsical
Or   naïve?

I believe
A statement to which
The young dedicate
And the older equivocate

I believe
A tightrope walk to an anchor
We all need.

25   HOTEL

Sign- night, light, bright, neon glare

Room 403

Brrm, brrm
Wheels of a car on carpet
Propelled by
Small hands

Room 303

With mum and dad
Again!
Why don't girls?
What is it about me?

Room 203

Disturbed sheets
Fumbling limbs
Some pain
Some pleasure
Conception

Room 103

Checked in alone
Man, middle aged
Suitcase, bourbon open
Tears
Abandoned by……..
Wanting, secretly
His youth
His mother
Comfort and security

Room 3

Next to sleeping wife
Rattling, rasping
Last

Lobby

The bar is shut
The porter dozes
The girl in reception, files
Season over.

Entrance

A taxi awaits
As the street scenes
Bustle on, and on,
And on.

26 DANCE

A rhythm that propels
Muscle memory, motion and meaning
We dance, we caress self's spirit
The whirl, the pulse, the joy of body.

27 LIVING WITH THE MACHINE

Unaware and unremebered
Continuous cohabitation
With my attachments

My Incubator
My light
My heat
My clothes
My food cooked and refrigerated

My entertainment
My treatments
My schooling
My work
My shopping
My communication
Linked and attached

As long as I can remember
A cyborg.

28 INTERNAL

Degraded and enlightened
Our mind talks
Dirty and pure
Spite and generosity
Only action
Tells.

Good and evil are
Choices appearing for selection
It is the decision device
That is
Us

29   DENIAL

My head
A bag of dust
Dry full of
Stats and nouns
Forgetting how
To be
Me:

Poet, Lover
Adventurer
Dream seeker
Child spirit
Man believer
Mystery to myself.

Forgotten me
In the box
Between work's weight
And responsibilities clasp

30 SIN

Why do we forget
The internal life of others?

Blinded by our
Internal lighting
Empathy diffuses.
People become
Irritants and enemies
Calculations;
Sub human
Even
Non human.
We all inhabit
Moments
of contemplated and random
Evil.

31   LETHE'S DRAUGHT

Nappy change
Ice Lolly fingers
Cry
Quick firm hands
Gentle

Mummy
Warm

Forgotten

32   CHRISTMAS MORN

Angels past
Sing towards lunch time's repast;
Children chase boxes bright
The labours of mother Hercules
Kitchen strife.
What was it that
Took us to today?
Babe in swaddling
Wonderment born of pain.

33   NOSTALGIA

Replacement reality
Retro wonder.

A soft focus mirror
Reflection a generous, warming haze.

A cracked bell
Tolling all the virtues.

Wished for home
Myth founded in fiction
Lost identity.

34   LOST SOULS

Faces bob up from the black flowing Lethe.
Momentarily reanimated but nameless.
Then carried into a dark slumberous distance.
Lost.
They submerge, forgotten again.

35 BY THE NUMBERS

2 – 1 = 1
Then 1 × 1 = 1
Then 1 / 1 = 1
Then 1 + 1 = 2
How many days have been this?

36   LETHE-WARDS

Nightingale, nightingale life your song drains.
Keat's made of you an opiate melodic;
Forgetfulness washing away deep pains.
A cure for the spiritual dyspeptic;
Ecstatic music as anaesthetic.
From the soul draining life and memory;
A verse conduit, vampire aesthetic.
Nightingale sing of fading sensory,
Though life's refrain drowns oblivion in memory.

37 FINDING THE WAY AGAIN

Can't breathe
Fear's weight
Blind Panic

Slowly, softly, quietly
Begin

Moving Lips;
Jesus thou son of David have mercy on me.
The blazing mind;
God be merciful to me a sinner.
The inner heart
Lord Jesus Christ, son of God, have mercy upon me.

Heart's drum eased
Cool water on parched tongue
Breathe

38   NEVERLAND

Tick tock
Peter Hook
Captain Pan
All the same
Boy and man

39 ANGELS AND DEVILS

Angel
Bringer
Messenger
Tool

Devil
Taker
Obfuscator
Fool

And we forget
And we regret

40 DUTCH COURAGE

Drink
For in your cups
Sups a fool forgotten,
Placed and buried.
An errant errand
To resuscitate a clown
Who fears less
And who you deny
Sober.

41 EROSION

Shops, home
Home, work
Work, home
Shops, home
Home, work
Work, work
Work, sometimes home
Shops.
Where am I?

42 CHANGES

Silver Birch
Autumnal
Dripping Leaves
Shedding intensity
Green no longer
Winter man
Aged, gnarled
Barren
Beautiful.

43 STANZA

Go not to Lethe
The Dull Isle
Sail onward
Under melancholy skies
This voyage is you.

44   FIRST LOVE PASSED

First love's kiss
Heated passion turned brittle
Now
Frozen shards shattered

" What happened to us ?"
Indelible silence

45   CAST IN A MIRROR DARKLY

Cast in a mirror darkly are dim reflections
Not of me
But a billion

Their lives rich inner sumptuous like mine
Their pain like mine
Their joy like mine
Their hope
Their inner vision and comfort

They are the infinitude of stars
The very dimension of the molecular
So many
Like me but not

We are unable to comprehend
A universe of sentience so multiplied
We are unable to transpose
Ourselves a billion times

So
The child starves
The numb butcher
The lonely fade
And
The stars are endless

46 NOSTALGIC

Ruritania your beauty awaits
Hidden now calling from far far away.
Mountain crisped morning air, snow kissed pates.
Sun hazing through forest pine starting the day;
The day I left that gilded sceptered realm.
A lost ship sailing, bow wave full of foam,
The compass point fading behind. My true spirits helm,
Ruritania , my lost perfect   home.

47　APOLLO

One melancholy summer
Warm sun
At ease
Where is Apollo?
Its bright wings taking to the moon.
Where is the soaring spirit?

Silence

Shy forgotten voice.
Beneath the moon.
We make money
The glory of money
Lots of money.

48   OLDER

No lion
No witch
A wardrobe

Aslan, oh Aslan
Come.

SHORT BIOGRAPHY:

Mark Isherwood was born in 1969 in Holbeach, Lincolnshire, England. He travelled extensively as a child and settled in Dorset, UK in his teens. He attended university and studied English and History at an undergraduate level and later management and education at a post graduate level. He has worked in a variety of post 16 education environments since 1997. He is a practicing Orthodox Christian and lives in London with his wife and two sons.

ABOUT THE WORK

Lethe was initially inspired by teaching Keats and preparing to teach Virgil. In particular the passages of the Aeniad based in the underworld and Keats's Ode to a Nightingale. The treatment of Lethe in both texts opened up creative possibilities around the notion of memory which serves as the connecting element which binds the 48 pieces together. The poet is a practicing Orthodox Christian and this forms the fundaments of the spiritual voice evident in many of the poems.

LETHE

By Mark Isherwood